John Muir

JOHN MUIR
(1838 – 1914)

QUOTATIONS

OF

John Muir

APPLEWOOD BOOKS
Carlisle, Massachusetts

Thank you for purchasing an Applewood book. Applewood reprints America's lively classics — books from the past that are still of interest to modern readers. For a free copy of our current catalog, please write or visit us at Applewood Books, 1 River Road, Carlisle, Massachusetts 01741.

www.awb.com

978-1-4290-9473-3

10 9 8 7 6 5 4 3 2

MANUFACTURED IN THE UNITED STATES OF AMERICA WITH AMERICAN-MADE MATERIALS

John Muir

JOHN MUIR was born in Dunbar, Scotland, on April 21, 1838, to Daniel and Ann Gilrye Muir, the third of eight children. John's father was a strict, devout man, and Muir's love of nature was possibly in resistance to this religious upbringing. In 1849, when John was eleven years old, the family emigrated to the United States, with his father choosing Wisconsin because of farming and business opportunities.

Young John was in love with nature and always felt more at home in the outdoors. As a youth he explored the hills and dales of Dunbar, and in America his attraction to the outdoors only increased. Once the family was settled, John began to widely roam about his new homeland. It was, he later wrote, his "baptism in Nature's warm heart." Nature nourished John Muir, mind, body, and soul.

Muir had a sharp mind and a natural gift for creating inventions. After attending the University of Wisconsin, he began his lifelong habit of going on excursions; he became a self-proclaimed "tramp." Recovering from a serious eye injury in 1867, he undertook a thousand-mile walk to the Gulf of Mexico from Indianapolis, a journey that introduced Muir to the wider world and what he called "the University of the Wilderness."

Going to California by steamer via the Isthmus of Panama in 1868, Muir ended up herding sheep in the Sierra Nevada mountains of California. John Muir found his life's purpose in the Sierra; he became the local expert, guiding visitors around Yosemite and writing articles about the mountains for national publications.

The 1880s saw Muir married, settled down, and raising a family while managing a 2,600-acre fruit ranch in Martinez, California. But domesticity did not stop him from his wanderings, with excursions to Alaska, Europe, and back to Yosemite. In 1889 Muir began his campaign to have Yosemite preserved for future generations, and the Yosemite National Park was created in 1890.

Muir became a tireless worker for governmental protection of wilderness areas. The end of the nineteenth century saw him form the Sierra Club. He crossed the country and traveled the world, including China and the Himalaya, spreading his gospel of preservation into the start of the twentieth century.

Age did not slow him down. Muir had three books published between 1911 and 1913. In 1911 he sailed up the Amazon River, traveled across South America, went to Africa to see Victoria Falls, and took a steamer up the Nile River.

With failing health the last two years of his life, in December 1914 Muir developed pneumonia and was admitted to the California Hospital in Los Angeles. He died on December 24, 1914. He was seventy-six years old.

QUOTATIONS

OF

John Muir

I never tried to abandon creeds or code of civilization; they went away of their own accord, melting and evaporating...without any effort.

– *Journal*, undated

John Muir

*O*ne of the finest snowstorms is raging now; the roaring wind thick with snow rushes cruelly through the desolate trees.

– Letter to Mrs. Ezra Carr, January 21, 1866

John Muir

*J*ohn Muir, Earth-planet, Universe.

– Muir's first *Journal* entry, July 1, 1867

John Muir

*T*he air [of the Sierra Nevada] was perfectly delicious, sweet enough for the breath of angels....I do not believe that Adam and Eve ever tasted better in their balmiest nook.

– Letter to Mrs. Ezra Carr, July 26, 1868

Sheep, like people, are ungovernable.

– *Journal*, June 16, 1869

John Muir

A most lovely day....Nature's song is daily enriched with the singing wings of flies, and the air is sweeter with the fragrance of added flowers.

– *Journal*, February 18, 1869

John Muir

Behold the King of glory, King Sequoia! Behold! Behold!

– Letter to Mrs. Ezra Carr, 1870

John Muir

The astronomer looks high, the geologist low. Who looks between on the surface of the earth? The farmer, I suppose, but too often he sees only grain, and of that only the mere bread-bushel-and-price side of it.

– *Journal*, undated

*A*s long as I live, I'll hear waterfalls and birds and winds sing. I'll interpret the rocks, learn the language of flood, storm and the avalanche. I'll acquaint myself with the glaciers and the wild gardens, and get as near the heart of the world as I can.

– *Journal*, 1871

John Muir

*T*he glorious crystal sediment [snow] was everywhere. From wall to wall of our beautiful temple, from meadow to sky was one finished unit of beauty...weighed in the celestial balances and found perfect.

– *Yosemite in Winter*, January 1, 1872

John Muir

*R*ocks and waters...are words of God and so are men. We all flow from one fountain Soul.

– Letter to Catherine Merrill, June 9, 1872

John Muir

*O*ne day's exposure to mountains is better than cartloads of books.

– *Journal*, 1872

$\mathcal{S}$o also the butter-and-milk habit has seized most people; bread without butter or coffee without milk is an awful calamity, as if everything before being put in our mouth must first be held under a cow. I know from long experience that...these things are unnecessary. One may take a little simple clean bread and have nothing to do these fine excursions but enjoy oneself. *Vide* Thoreau.

– Journal, 1872

John Muir

$\mathcal{Y}$ou cannot be content with last year's baptism. 'Twas only a sprinkle. Come be immersed....You will lose...nothing but civilized sins.

– Letter to Ralph Waldo Emerson, 1872

John Muir

$\mathcal{L}$iving artificially in towns, we are sickly, and never come to know ourselves.

– Explorations in the Greater Tuolumne Canyon, 1873

I used to envy the father of our race, dwelling as he did in contact with the new-made fields and plants of Eden; but I do so no more, because I have discovered that I also live in "creation's dawn."
– *Explorations in the Greater Tuolumne Canyon*, 1873

John Muir

*T*he life of a mountaineer seems to be particularly favorable to the development of soul-life, as well as limb-life, each receiving abundance of exercise and abundance of food.
– *Explorations in the Greater Tuolumne Canyon*, 1873

John Muir

*B*etween every two pine trees there is a door leading to a new way of life.
– Marginal notation in Muir's copy of Emerson's *Prose Works*, Volume I

John Muir

*T*he mountains are calling and I must go.
– Letter to Sarah Muir Galloway, September 3, 1873

I know that our bodies were made to thrive only in pure air, and the scenes in which pure air is found.
– *Journal*, September 1874

I care to live only to entice people to look at Nature's loveliness.
– Letter to Mrs. Ezra Carr, October 7, 1874

*W*e little know how much wildness there is in us. Only a few generations separate us from our grandfathers that were savage as wolves.... Savageness is natural, civilization is strained and unnatural.
– *Journal*, November 29, 1874

*N*ature is a good mother.
– *Overland Monthly*, 1875

*P*lants, animals and stars are all kept in place, bridled along appointed ways, with one another, and through the midst of one another—killing and being killed, eaten and being eaten, in harmonious proportions and quantities.

– *Overland Monthly*, 1875

John Muir

I would advise sitting from morning till night under some willow bush on the river bank where there is a wide view. This will be "doing the valley" far more effectively than riding along trails in constant motion from point to point.

– *San Francisco Daily Evening Bulletin*, June 14, 1875

John Muir

*N*o synonym for God is so perfect as Beauty.

– *Journal*, June 26, 1875

John Muir

*A*n owl, the prince of lunatics. Health in his soft..."*too-whoo-hoo-hoo*."

– *Journal*, August 1875

*G*oing to mountains is going home.
– *San Francisco Daily Evening Bulletin*, August 3, 1875

John Muir

*T*he hall and the theater and the church have been invented, and compulsory education. Why not add compulsory recreation?
– *Journal*, November 12, 1875

John Muir

*C*onstancy of the feelings which Nature excites is the most enduring of all. Love is only intensified with absence. "Familiarity breeds contempt" is the meanest of all aphorisms.
– *Journal*, August 1876

John Muir

*I*n every walk with nature one receives far more than he seeks.
– *San Francisco Daily Evening Bulletin*, July 19, 1877

I should like to sketch one of these Alaska summer days, however imperfect the sketch must be. It is a day without night, for it begins and ends at midnight, which is the low noon of the great round day.

– *Journal*, July 10, 1879

John Muir

I t is too often found that in attempting to Christianize savages they become very nearly nothing, lose their wild instincts, and gain a hymnbook, without the means of living....Then they mope and doze and die on the outskirts of civilization like tamed eagles in barnyard corners, with blunt talons, blunt bills and clipped wings.

– *Journal*, July 1879

John Muir

O nly by going alone in silence, without baggage, can one truly get into the heart of the wilderness. All other travel is mere dust and hotels and baggage and chatter.

– Letter to Louisa Strentzel Muir, July 1888

When one is alone at night in the depths of the woods, the stillness is at once awful and sublime. Every leaf seems to speak. One gets close to Nature, and the love of beauty grows as it cannot in the distractions of a camp.

– *Journal*, August 9, 1888

John Muir

Doubly happy, however, is the man to whom the lofty mountain tops are within reach, for the lights that shine there illumine all that lies below.

– *Washington and the Puget Sound*, 1888–1890

John Muir

Take a course of good water and air, and in the eternal youth of Nature you may renew your own. Go quietly alone; no harm will befall you.

– *Picturesque California*, 1888–1890

John Muir

Happy will be the men who, having the power and the love and the benevolent forecast to [create a park] will do it. The trees and their lovers… will rise up and call them blessed.

– *Picturesque California*, 1888–1890

*M*e the poetico-trampo-geologist-bot &
ornith—natural etc. etc - ! - ! - !!
– Letter to Robert Underwood Johnson, September 13, 1889

John Muir

*A*ll the wild world is beautiful, and it
matters but little where we go, to highlands or
lowlands, woods or plains, on the sea or land...
everywhere and always we are in God's eternal
beauty and love.
– *Journal*, June 1890

John Muir

*W*hen we are with Nature we are awake.
– *Journal*, June, 1890

John Muir

*T*o the Indian mind all nature was instinct with
deity. A spirit was embodied in every mountain,
stream and waterfall.
– *Journal*, July 1890

*M*ost people are *on* the world, not in it—
have no conscious sympathy or relationship to
anything about them—undiffused, separate, and
rigidly alone like marbles of polished stone.

– *Journal*, July 1890

I have always enjoyed the hearty society of a
snowstorm.

– *Journal*, July 19, 1890

*T*he clearest way into the Universe is through a
forest wilderness.

– *Journal*, July 1890

I never saw a discontented tree. They grip the
ground as though they liked it.

– *Journal*, July 1890

*L*et our law-givers then make haste before it
is too late to set apart [the South Fork of King's
River] for the recreation and well-being of
humanity, and all the world will rise up and call
them blessed.

– *Century Magazine*, November 1891

Went through lovely, ferny flowery woods...
and laid flowers on Thoreau's and Emerson's
graves....I think it is the most beautiful grave-
yard I ever saw....Sweet, kindly Mother Earth
has taken them back to her bosom whence they
came. I did not imagine I would be so moved at
sight of the resting places of these grand men as
I found I was.

– *Journal*, 1893

John Muir

How glorious a greeting the sun gives the
mountains!

– *The Mountains of California*, 1894

John Muir

Go where you may within the bounds of California, mountains are ever in sight, charming and
glorifying every landscape.

– *The Mountains of California*, 1894

*A*ccidents in the mountains are less common than in the lowlands, and these mountain mansions are decent, delightful, and even divine places to die in, compared with the doleful chambers of civilization.

– *The Mountains of California*, 1894

John Muir

*F*resh beauty opens one's eyes whenever it is readily seen, but the very abundance and completeness of the common beauty that besets our steps prevents its being absorbed and appreciated.

– *The Mountains of California*, 1894

John Muir

*D*ark. The rain-clouds in wondrous depth and fruitfulness. It seems marvelous that so much rain can be stored in the sky.

– *Journal*, January 20, 1895

John Muir

*N*ature is always lovely, invincible, glad, whatever is done and suffered by her creatures. All scars she heals, whether in rocks or water or sky or hearts.

– *Journal*, March 24, 1895

God never made an ugly landscape. All that the sun shines on is beautiful, so long as it is wild.
– *The National Parks and Forest Reservations*, 1895

John Muir

The battle we have fought, and are still fighting for the forests is part of the eternal conflict between right and wrong.
– *The National Parks and Forest Reservations*, 1895

John Muir

Walked over the hills....How the wind did surge and hiss and rustle and shout in the rocks and trees and grass! How the tall grain waved... with racing enthusiasm, and how the wild oats danced and rippled and clapped their spikelets like happy hands in a passion of joy!
– *Journal*, May 8, 1896

John Muir

Death is as natural as life, sorrow as joy. Through pain and death come all our blessings, life and immortality.
– Letter to Julia Merrill Moores, July 25, 1900

The wrong done to trees, wrongs of every sort, are done in the darkness of ignorance and unbelief, for when light comes, the heart of the people is always right.

– *Journal*, 1900

John Muir

I urged Emerson to stay [and camp out underneath the sequoia trees]. "You are yourself a sequoia," I said. "Stop and get acquainted with your big brethren."

– *Our National Parks*, 1901

John Muir

None of nature's landscapes are ugly so long as they are wild.

– *Our National Parks*, 1901

John Muir

The forests of America, however slighted by man, must have been a great delight to God; for they were the best he has ever planted.

– *Our National Parks*, 1901

*C*limb the mountains and get their good tidings. Nature's peace will flow into you as sunshine flows into trees. The winds will blow their own freshness into you, and the storms their energy, while cares will drop off like autumn leaves.
– *Our National Parks*, 1901

John Muir

*T*housands of tired, nerve-shaken, over-civilized people are beginning to find out that going to the mountains is going home; that wilderness is a necessity.
– *Our National Parks*, 1901

John Muir

*H*ow many hearts with warm, red blood in them are beating under cover of the woods, and how many teeth and eyes are shining! A multitude of animal people...are as busy about their own affairs as we are about ours.
– *Our National Parks*, 1901

John Muir

*T*he dawn, as in all the pure, dry, desert country, is ineffably beautiful; and when the first level sunbeams sting the domes and spires...rocks and hearts alike, awake and sing the new-old song of creation.
–*Century Magazine*, 1902

I had a perfectly good time with [President Theodore Roosevelt] and the mountains. I never before had a more interesting, hearty and manly companion.

– Letter to Louisa Strentzel Muir, May 19, 1903

John Muir

*H*appy the man to whom every tree is a friend—who loves them, sympathizes with them....We may love them all and carry them about with us in our hearts.

– *Journal*, September 4, 1908

John Muir

*T*here is no estimating the wit and wisdom concealed and latent in our lower fellow mortals until made manifest by profound experiences; for it is through suffering that dogs as well as saints are developed and made perfect.

– *Stickeen*, 1909

John Muir

*N*o right way is easy in this rough world. We must risk our lives to save them.

– *Stickeen*, 1909

*N*one of Stickeen's friends know what finally became of him....His fate is wrapped in mystery. Doubtless he has left this world...and gone to another. But he will not be forgotten. To me Stickeen is immortal.

– *Stickeen*, 1909

John Muir

*L*ie down among the pines for a while, then get to plain, pure, white-love work.

– Letter to Mrs. J. D. Hooker, September 1911

John Muir

*S*o extravagant is Nature with her choicest treasures, spending plant beauty as she spends sunshine, pouring it forth into land and sea, garden and desert.

– *My First Summer in the Sierra*, 1911

John Muir

*T*he whole wilderness seems to be alive and familiar, full of humanity. The very stones seem talkative, sympathetic, brotherly.

– *My First Summer in the Sierra*, 1911

When we try to pick out anything by itself, we find it hitched to everything else in the Universe.

– *My First Summer in the Sierra*, 1911

John Muir

Good walkers can go anywhere in these hospitable mountains without artificial ways.

– *Letter to Howard Palmer, December 12, 1912*

John Muir

Everybody needs beauty as well as bread, place to play in and pray in, where Nature may heal and cheer and give strength to body and soul alike.

– *The Yosemite*, 1912

John Muir

This national beauty-hunger is made manifest…in our magnificent National Parks….Nature's sublime wonderlands, the admiration and joy of the world.

– *The Yosemite*, 1912

John Muir

These temple destroyers, devotees of ravaging commercialism, seem to have a perfect contempt for Nature, and instead of lifting their eyes to the God of the mountains, lift them to the Almighty Dollar.

– *The Yosemite*, 1912

26

*A*ll Nature's wildness tells the same story: the shocks and outbursts of earthquakes, volcanoes, geysers, roaring thundering waves and floods, the silent uprush of sap in plants, storms of every sort, each and all are the orderly beauty-making love-beats of Nature's heart.

– *Century Magazine*, 1912

*W*hen I was a boy in Scotland I was fond of everything that was wild, and all my life I've been growing fonder and fonder of wild places and wild creatures.

– *The Story of My Boyhood and Youth*, 1913

*T*his sudden plash into pure wilderness— baptism in Nature's warm heart—how utterly happy it made us! Oh that glorious Wisconsin wilderness!

– *The Story of My Boyhood and Youth*, 1913

*A*lthough I was four years at the University, I did not take the regular course of studies, but... was far from satisfied with what I had learned.... Anyhow, I wandered away on a glorious botanical and geological excursion, which has lasted for nearly fifty years.

– *The Story of My Boyhood and Youth*, 1913

*S*urely all God's people, however serious or savage, great or small, like to play. Whales and elephants, dancing, humming gnats, and invisibly small mischievous microbes—all are warm with divine radium and must have lots of fun in them.

– *The Story of My Boyhood and Youth*, 1913

*F*rom the top of a hill...I gained a last, wistful, lingering view of the beautiful University grounds....But I was only leaving one University for another, the Wisconsin University for the University of the Wilderness.

– *The Story of My Boyhood and Youth*, 1913

I only went out for a walk, and finally concluded to stay out till sundown, for going out, I found, was really going in.

– *Journal*, circa 1913

John Muir

*C*louds. Think of the cooling shadows of summer clouds which benevolent Nature spreads over her darling forests and gardens—summer shadows of wonderful depth and brilliancy like the wings of a mother bird over her young.

–*Journal*, circa 1913

John Muir

*T*he touch of invisible things is in snow, the lightest, tenderest of all material. I have lain... with my face to the snowflakes falling like the touch of fingertips upon my eyes.

– *Journal*, circa 1913

John Muir

*T*he very thought of this Alaska garden is a joyful exhilaration.

– *Travels in Alaska*, 1915

Keep close to Nature's heart...and break clean away, once in awhile, and climb a mountain or spend a week in the woods. Wash your spirit clean.

– *Alaska Days with John Muir*, 1915

John Muir

When we contemplate the whole globe as one great dewdrop...flying through space with other stars all surging and shining together as one, the whole Universe appears as one infinite storm of beauty.

– *Travels in Alaska*, 1915

John Muir

My fire was in all its glory about midnight, and, having made a bark shed to shelter me from the rain and partially dry my clothing, I had nothing to do but look and listen and join the trees in their hymns and prayers.

– *Travels in Alaska*, 1915

John Muir

The world, we are told, was made especially for man—a presumption not supported by all the facts.

– *A Thousand-Mile Walk to the Gulf*, 1916

The Universe would be incomplete without man; but it would also be incomplete without the smallest transmicroscopic creature that dwells beyond our conceitful eyes and knowledge.
– *A Thousand-Mile Walk to the Gulf*, 1916

John Muir

How imperishable are all the impressions that ever vibrate one's life! We cannot forget anything. Memories may escape the action of will... but when stirred by the right influence...they flash into full stature and life with everything in place.
– *A Thousand-Mile Walk to the Gulf*, 1916

John Muir

Why should man value himself as more than a small part of the one great unit of creation? And what creature of all that the Lord has taken the pains to make is not essential to the completeness of...the cosmos?
– *A Thousand-Mile Walk to the Gulf*, 1916

John Muir

One touch of nature makes all the world kin.
– *The Cruise of the Corwin*, 1917

*E*merson was the most serene, majestic sequoia-like soul I ever met. His smile was as sweet and calm as morning light on mountains....He was as sincere as the trees, his eye sincere as the sun.
– *Journal*, undated

John Muir

*I*t is my faith that every flower enjoys the air it breathes. Wordsworth, Professors Wagner, French and Darwin claim that plants have minds, are conscious of their existence, feel pain and have memories.
– *Journal*, undated

John Muir

*M*yriads of rejoicing, living creatures, daily, hourly, perhaps every moment, sink into death's arms, dust to dust, spirit to spirit—waited on, watched over, noticed only by the Maker, each arriving at its own heaven-dealt destiny....All the merry dwellers of the trees and streams, and the myriad swarms of the air, called into life by the sunbeam of a summer morning, go home through death...all alike pass on and away under the law of death and love.
– *Journal*, undated

John Muir